Snakes

by Annabelle Lynch

W
FRANKLIN WATTS
LONDON·SYDNEY

First published in 2014 by
Franklin Watts
338 Euston Road
London NW1 3BH

Franklin Watts Australia
Level 17/207 Kent Street
Sydney NSW 2000

Picture credits:
John Cancalosi/Alamy: 10. Daexto/Dreamstime: 6.
Caleb Foster/Shutterstock: 12. Isselee/Dreamstime: 4.
Heiko Kiera/Shutterstock: 1, 9. Thomas Marent/
Minden Pictures/FLPA: 18. Mgkuijpers/Dreamstime:
17. Mgkuijpers/Shutterstock: 21. Sproicky/
Shutterstock: 13. Coy St Clair/Dreamstime: 5. Ryan
Stevenson/Dreamstime: 15.

Every attempt has been made to clear copyright.
Should there be any inadvertent omission please
apply to the publisher for rectification.

 A CIP catalogue record for this book is
available from the British Library.

Dewey number: 597.96

ISBN 978 1 4451 2915 0 (hbk)
ISBN 978 1 4451 3049 1 (pbk)
Library eBook ISBN 978 1 44512921 1

Series Editor: Julia Bird
Series Advisor: Catherine Glavina
Series Designer: Peter Scoulding

Printed in China

Franklin Watts is a division of Hachette Children's Books,
an Hachette UK company. www.hachette.co.uk

Contents

The words in **bold** can be found in the glossary.

What are snakes?

Snakes are long, thin **reptiles**. They don't have legs and their skin is covered in tiny **scales**.

Snakes are cold-blooded. They move to hot places to warm up and cool places to cool down.

scales

Where are snakes found?

Snakes are found all over the world, from green jungles to sandy deserts. There are no snakes in Antarctica. It is too cold for them to live there.

Some snakes, like this banded sea krait, even live in the sea.

Hatching from eggs

Most snakes **hatch** from eggs. The mother lays the eggs in a warm place, then leaves. The baby snakes look after themselves.

Snakes have a sharp tooth called an egg tooth which helps them tear through the eggshell.

Shedding skin

Over their lifetime, snakes **moult** or lose their skin many times. This allows their bodies to grow.

Snakes often rub up against something rough to help them moult.

Eating

Snakes are **carnivores**. They eat other animals, insects, birds and lizards. Snakes have bendy **jaws** which help them eat things much bigger than themselves.

Snakes use their forked tongues to 'taste' the air around them, and to track down food.

Getting around

Snakes have strong **muscles** which they use to move around. Snakes can slither, climb, swim and jump. Some snakes can even **glide** through the air!

A snake's scales help them to grip anything, even sand.

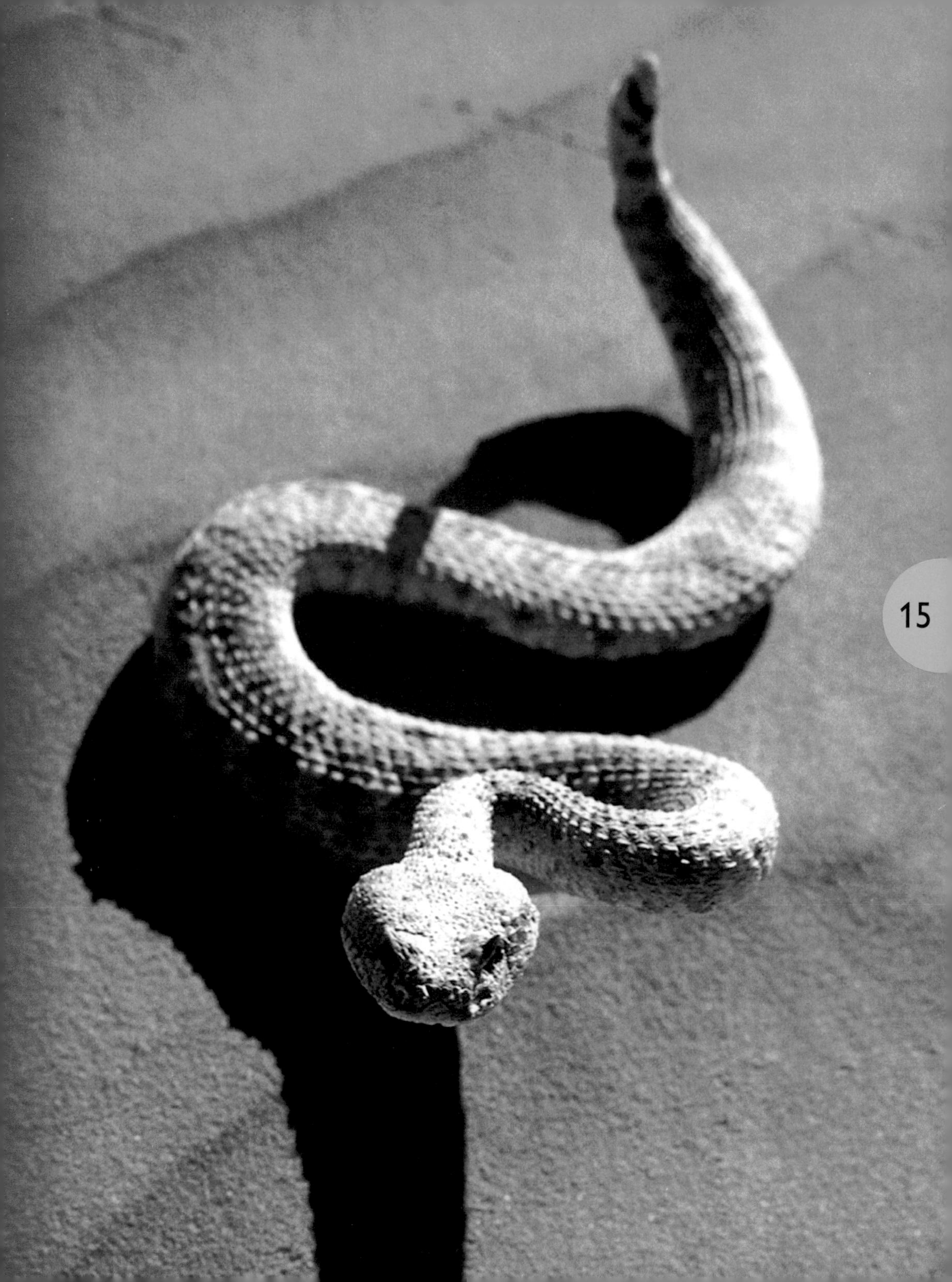

Venomous snakes

Some snakes, such as vipers and cobras, use **venom** to harm or kill their **prey**. They put it into their prey's body through their fangs.

Snake venom can be used to make medicine to treat snake bites.

18

squeezing Snakes

Some snakes snatch their prey with their teeth, then wrap their body around it. They squeeze tighter until the prey stops breathing. Then the snake eats it up!

The huge green anaconda can squeeze prey as big as deer and crocodiles to death.

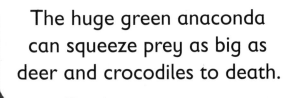

In danger

In some places, snakes are at risk. People use their skin to make shoes and handbags. The wild places where snakes live are also disappearing.

Snakes may seem dangerous, but they are more at risk from people than we are from them.

Glossary

carnivore – animals that only eat meat

glide – to slide through the air

hatch – to break out from inside an egg

jaws – the mouth and teeth

moult – to lose skin, hair or feathers

muscles – parts of our body that help us move

prey – an animal that is eaten by another animal

reptiles – cold-blooded creatures that have scales and lay eggs

scales – small pieces of hard skin

venom – a type of poison

Websites:

http://animals.nationalgeographic.com/animals/photos/snakes/

http://www.kidzone.ws/lw/snakes/

Every effort has been made by the Publishers to ensure that the websites are suitable for children, and that they contain no inappropriate or offensive material. However, because of the nature of the Internet, it is impossible to guarantee that the contents of these sites will not be altered. We strongly advise that Internet access is supervised by a responsible adult.

Quiz

1. Why are there no snakes in Antarctica?

2. What do snakes use their egg tooth for?

3. Why do snakes moult?

4. What do snakes eat?

5. Give an example of how a snake can move.

6. How do snakes put venom into their prey's body?

The answers are on page 24

Answers

1. It is too cold for them to live there
2. To tear through eggshell
3. So that their bodies can grow
3. Other animals, insects, birds and lizards
5. Slither, climb, swim, jump, glide
6. Through their fangs

Index